(cacharel)

© Assouline Publishing
601 West 26th Street, 18th floor
New York, NY 10001
USA
Tél.: 212 989-6810   Fax: 212 647-0005
www.assouline.com

ISBN : 2-84323-403-4

Translated from French by Bernard Wooding

Color separation : GEGM (France)
Printing by Grafiche Milani (Italy)

(cacharel)

JÉROMINE SAVIGNON

ASSOULINE

I t is spring 1968. Not everything is permissible yet, but everything is going to become possible. Gérard Grandval, architect of the "realist utopias" and designer of the "flower houses" in Créteil, has just designed an astonishing new concept in offices between Place de la République and the Canal Saint-Martin in Paris. Located in a disused printing works on the Rue du Faubourg-du-Temple, it seems to boldly embody all the dreams of the moment. The vast, white-painted, windowless interior is occupied by a series of bubbles made of colored polyester. These fully equipped work cocoons in plain red or Klein blue have wide portholes and look for all the world like space ships. Facing them is the totally transparent director's office, which is like a giant aquarium. Here, the walls, table and telephone — everything except the collapsible columnar armchair in red and white polyester — is made of Plexiglas. Secret agent? Famous advertising executive? Avant-garde bank manager? In fact, this is the office of Jean Bousquet, founder of the Jean Cacharel label.

The audacity of this futuristic office was in perfect accord with the sensibility of this avant-garde designer at a time when the Sixties youth culture was about to explode. At that time, a wind of excitement was blowing through the fashion world. An experimental euphoria characterized by optimism and a carefree attitude emerged. This irresistible "new wave" brought with it the slightly naïve idea of a world free from conflict, of a world wavering between wonder and reality in a return to innocence that was almost childlike.

●

In the whirlwind of this radical change in values and the sudden emergence of young people, fashion — the kind of fashion that was worn, the fashion of life and of the street — was caught between conformity and freedom. In this realm, fashion designers were no longer the ultimate reference. But the burgeoning ready-to-wear sector, based on the search for style, still remained implicitly influenced by notions of smartness and elegance, the convention of the suit and the well-cut coat. But young women had changed; they now dreamed of simplicity, genuine freshness, a type of fashion that was pretty, easy and cheerful, as well as being a little sexy, a type of fashion designed above all to give pleasure.

More than any other company, Cacharel was able to give concrete expression to these desires, to turn a dream of lightness into a sort of institution, producing a "ready-to-please-shock" for attractive college girls that would become the symbol of an entire generation.

To begin with, the story of Cacharel is a simple story of small items, of short gabardine skirts, neat little blouses like boy's shirts, soft, colorful fabrics that were easy to wear. The best-known creation, though, was a reinterpretation of a man's shirt, the famous *chemisier crépon*: "the Cacharel." This was an incredibly daring design. the *crépon*, a crease-resistant but humble material, had up until then only been used for women's underwear. Attracted to its basic, functional character, Jean Bousquet immediately saw its potential. Thanks to its stretchiness and its already wrinkled quality, the *crépon* made it possible to considerably reduce the structure of a garment and to get rid of the traditional bust darts. It was at this time that young women were casting off their bras, and the *chemisier crépon* replaced them to some extent. It was a genuinely creative design because it involved using an existing material in a new way, offering it in a functional cut, with straight lines, turned up sleeves, and ingenious buttons. It was a piece of clothing made for the fantastical body of an androgynous adolescent whose icons at the time were Jane Birkin and Françoise Dorléac. The shape was new and gave rise to a new attitude, a revolution in the way people moved, giving rise to a fashion that was more essential, perhaps, than the miniskirt. "Sweet, simple and sexy", this blouse was the revolutionary clothing archetype of the Sixties. Plain or with acid caramel stripes, "Cacharel crépon" was the uniform of the summer of 1965. People would say "It's a Cacharel," the way people talk of a pair of Levi's or a Burberry. And in *Inventaire 66*, Michel Delpech sang "A miniskirt, two Courrèges boots . . . a Cacharel."

But Jean Bousquet was already looking for a new idea. A mythical piece of clothing, but also a pivotal one, the *chemisier crépon* heralded new dreams that were about to unfold. With its invigorating, youthful overtones, it seemed to be the quintessence of a fashion concept that was in perfect accord with the moment and the futuristic offices of the Rue Faubourg-du-Temple. But the transparency and intangibility of this item led imperceptibly to other, younger, more aerial images: those of the dream of a woman yet to be discovered. Intuitively, Jean Bousquet sensed that he had to embrace this notion of lightness more fully. So he invented the Liberty fabric.

Liberty and Cacharel — the two names are inseparable. But who today can say what Liberty was really about? The history of an

English garden? Fresh cotton for well-behaved children? Little flowers in soft watercolor hues? It was all of those things, of course. But above all it was an adventure — a rather extraordinary one in the context of the nineteenth century — the adventure of an Englishman of Corsican origin, Arthur Lasenby Liberty.

●

In 1875, he opened on Regent Street, under the name of Liberty, a sort of bazaar, a treasure chest, where people could find all the Oriental things that were fashionable at the time: Japanese curios, Indian silks, Turkish velvet, cashmere items and exotic trinkets. Initially bought directly in Japan, China and India, the household fabrics were soon being made in London. Arthur Liberty made the most beautiful silks and cottons and the finest cashmeres on his own looms. Drawing heavily on the Oriental motifs — stylized interlacing and flowers — of the first imported silks, his fabrics were given their distinctive pastel hues — pink, tea, jade green, sand beige, delicate blue — the Art Nouveau colors that quickly became known as the "Liberty colors" throughout the world. Arthur Liberty became famous. His "East India House" became place of fashion. Conscious of his role as former of tastes in a variety of fields, he added a decorative furniture range, and was an occasional theater costume designer. He even turned his hand to clothes design, entrusting this new department to Edward Godwin, architect of Oscar Wilde and Whistler and costume historian. Godwin was an ardent follower of the Aesthetic Movement that was all the rage at the time and he worshiped the Greek tunic. Under his direction, Liberty fostered a return to flexibility, to a more natural feel. Around 1884, the company offered a range of what were called "Aesthetic" dresses — loose, fluid clothes more or less inspired by the free Greek shape. "Exquisite dresses," wrote a journalist of the time — exquisite above all because of the excellent quality of the fabrics and the delicate harmony of the colors. Soon, a Liberty store opened in Paris, in the Opéra neighborhood. It is said that Proust bought his *lavallières* there and that *fin de siècle* mothers could find charming smock dresses for their little girls in the catalogues.

Liberty is synonymous with the artistic upheavals of the period and their avant-garde manifestations. Initially a forum for the Aesthetic Movement, it later drew Pre-Raphaelite artists like Burne-Jones, William Morris, Alma-Tadema and Dante Gabriel Rossetti. A little later, Arthur Liberty became an ardent supporter of Art Nouveau and the philosophy of the Arts and Crafts Movement. There was an osmosis, a general climate that served to enrich the refined graphic design of the Liberty textiles. The motifs — lotuses, irises, jasmine and the famous peacock's feather — were initially in an Oriental, William Morris style, but from 1890 they began to acquire a bucolic freshness and a childlike naivety. Birds, wildflowers, poppies and daisies appeared. As a result, for a few decades Liberty became a unique place where art and fashion came together and interacted to create a style, the Liberty style.

When its founder died in 1917, Liberty seemed to lose something of its soul and no longer had its finger on the pulse of the new trends of the period. And in 1932, the company inappropriately entrusted its fashion department to the aging Poiret.

Yet Liberty's textiles retained their prestige, adhering unswervingly to Oriental and floral decorative tradition. The most famous Liberty textile is undoubtedly the "Tana Lawn," a superb cotton fabric from the Sudan, the finest, silkiest in the world, with an inimitable glazed finish. Large quantities were supplied for the young princesses Elizabeth and Margaret. But by the spring of

1968, this fabric, despite its extraordinary quality, seemed to have become forgotten by the fashion world. Sold by the yard, it was generally only found in the nursery, in the smocks of the immaculate little girls of the London gentry and of the wealthy neighborhoods of Paris, and in the traditional outfits worn at smart marriages. Its floral motifs and soft colors were imbued with a slightly dated feel of outmoded elegance such as might be found at a game of croquet in an English garden. In short, it was an old-fashioned fabric. And yet it was with this material that Jean Bousquet set about founding the legend that is Cacharel.

a fter the success that he made out of the *crépon* of ladies' underwear, he looked for other fabrics that would provide new sensations of lightness. He no doubt remembered the colorful, summery images that he brought back from a trip to the Caribbean in 1962 that marked him deeply. When Liberty's agent in Paris presented his collection to him, his decision was instantaneous: this was the fabric for Cacharel. In one look he grasped all its potential. For this style, with its thick, dense, English overtones, for this magical cotton that was as soft as silk and light as *crépon*, and that was easy to maintain, there had to be a market. All that was needed was to bring it back to life, a life that was already beginning to take shape in the fingers that were rubbing the "Tana Lawn." fabric. One of Jean Bousquet's biggest talents has been his instinct for knowing what kind of clothing could come out of a fabric. The decision was made: the next Cacharel shirts would be made out of Liberty fabric.

At the time, there was a young girl who had recently started working at Cacharel. Her name was Corinne Sarrut and she had just started out as a fashion designer, a profession that was in its infancy at the time. Slender, with long, light brown hair, big green eyes like those of Scarlett O'Hara, a touch of the hippy and a hint of the well-behaved boarder, she was Jean Bousquet's sister-in-law. On leaving the Ecole des Beaux-Arts, she did an internship at Cacharel, although she didn't take it too seriously at the time. She dressed prettily, wearing the clothes she felt like wearing, odd little "things," "bits and pieces," gorgeous mixtures of little turquoise or pastel-colored Shetland wool pullovers, printed sateen, grandma's shirts and old clothes picked up at flea markets. In fact, she embodied the ideal client he was dreaming of and he suggested that she design the summer 1967 collection. Corinne stayed.

Subsequently, as Cacharel's official designer, she simply went on to create, from one collection to the next, the kind of fashion that she liked. And the Liberty is the most faithful and charming reflection of this.

"What interested me at the time," recalls Corinne today, "was all that went with the hippy movement, the attitude, the emancipation. I was part of this generation. We were all part of it. It wasn't political, it was a lifestyle[1]". Like all the young "flower people" of the post-1968 period, she was swept along by the happy, fabulous illusion of a gentler way of life, the freedom to express one's emotions and fulfill one's desires to the full. She saw *Hair*, of course. She loved clogs, large necklaces, Indian headscarves, the little "bells" with flowers pulled down over the eyes and the retro charm of the dresses her mother wore in photos taken in the 1930s. She liked René Clair, Renoir, Truffaut, Claude Jade in *Baisers Volés* and André Breton's cult film *Peter Ibbitson*, which celebrated in images the supreme power of dreams, dreams as the axiom of the artist.

Corinne Sarrut inevitably fell in love with the Liberty style. Instinctively, she transposed a few elements of the hippy philosophy to her conception of cotton. What stimulated her imagination was the idea of a cotton that was light, natural, slightly rustic, very fresh and evocative of a young woman, combining a traditional romantic English feel with "Peace and Love" overtones. She was attracted to drawings with fine lines, naïvely rendered little flowers and scenes that were straight out of the *Malheurs de Sophie* or a book of illustrations by Kate Greenaway: "What was pretty about Liberty was their very childish, delicate, refined prints[1]". Then there was the excitement, exhilarating for a designer, of using a fabric that had been consigned to the "children's range" in order to clothe young women of twenty who, for the first time ever perhaps, wanted their very own fashion and refused to go straight from the school uniform to the starchy conventional women's suit as worn by their mothers.

●

Jean Bousquet, an "astute businessman who thought simultaneously in artistic, social and business terms[2]", knew that it was time for the company to move on, to distance itself a little from its sportswear range and the futuristic image of the offices in the Rue du Faubourg-du-Temple. To achieve this shift toward a more romantic feel, he gave his sister-in-law free rein to use her imagination and sensibility.

Using the Liberty style, Corinne would without — thinking about it too analytically, almost by playing around, and yet with infinite grace — provide the answer to the unarticulated rejection and the new expectations of the period — both hers and those of eighteen-to twenty-year-olds, "her kindred spirits, her sisters."

"Let us take you by the hand. Above all, keep your eyes wide open. You are about to discover the fashion of your holidays. A fashion that is simple, free and full of *joie de vivre*. There are sensible little school dresses that are flexible, light and short, very short — as they should be, because the days are getting longer. There are long flowing dresses for the evening. You will like the muted colors: khakis, browns, dark reds, old pinks. You will take a liking to the hearts, birds, butterflies, flowers and stars. What a pretty summer it will be!"

This invitation to a voyage in Cacharel's summer 1971 collection wonderfully captures the spirit of the fashion being created by Corinne Sarrut at the time. With Cacharel's first little dresses for the summer of 1970, she had already dressed every woman in Liberty fabric. The fineness of this fabric, which permitted a cut that was closer to the body, enabled her to develop to an extreme degree the idea — hers and that of Jean Bousquet — of lightness. Always keep things as light as possible, take the adolescent lines and volumes as far as possible. The result was the endearing, graceful silhouette of a woman-child who had barely emerged from the ambiguous dreams of the unattractive age; a seductive doll, half Agnès, half Lolita, who had escaped from a painting by Balthus; a girl-flower who does not live in the past but who still hums nursery rhymes, which she has not forgotten.

From one collection and one season to the next, Corinne dressed her according to the mood of the moment and the images that came to her. With Corinne, "little Cacharel" had fun: in a mini-dress with puff sleeves; in a deceptively ingenuous pinafore with little Liberty flowers, round neckline, long straight sleeves, and short pleated skirt and which could be undone from top to bottom thanks to a profusion of tiny buttons. Sometimes she was wrapped up like Russian doll or, like Cyd Charisse in *The Bandwagon*, she would make her loose dress with its fine pleats dance in the wind. One summer she even caught herself dreaming of the 1930s.

And as ever there was lots and lots of Liberty. There were soft, nuanced hues and subdued, refined harmonies. There were dense prints with tightly packed motifs, bunches of flowers, fruit, a Japanese landscape, cashmere palmettes, a "Cunard" print that conjured up cruises, and even a very Art Deco, jazzy silk print.

The fabric collections that Liberty provided were occasionally heavy and a little conventional. With the help of Corinne Sarrut, Jean Bousquet took them in hand. Together they went to London, searched through the archives and unearthed some very old, long-forgotten drawings. They had them reprinted, re-colored the range using colors from the current collection and secured exclusive rights to them. Thanks to a transformed red, Liberty became Cacharel. In this adaptation, Corinne demonstrated an understanding of both the material and the motifs. Thanks to this secret union, this complicity even, she succeeded in breaking with the "sober pastel" aspect of the fabric, turning it into something different for the young women of her age and, beyond that, creating a whole style. Prior to Cacharel, nobody had asserted in such a strong way the presence of a print in a brand, establishing it as a "fashion object." From this time on, it was through Liberty that the "little Cacharels" would pursue their dream of natural insouciance and light happiness. It is no coincidence that Cacharel has always made people think of Liberty.

Corinne Sarrut's collaboration with Liberty is clear. Beyond the name itself, flapping like a flag, the romance of this fabric was a vehicle for all the fantasies of a generation, as represented by hippy music and the female heroines of the novels popular in France at the time — *Petites Filles modèles* and *Claudine à l'école*.

The dress that best encapsulates Corinne's work with the Liberty fabrics, the one that has remained her favorite to this day, is the gypsy dress, the one worn by the character of Aurora in the film *Le Genou de Claire*. It is a sort of jerkin, with a U-shaped neckline, clinging closely to the narrow bust before fanning out, low on the hips and down to the feet, in a voluminous swirling, flowing skirt. It is a joyful dress, a dress for the *Sacre du printemps*, a dress that seems to take you by the hand to lead you, crowned with flowers and bare-footed, to an improvised dance at a hippy beach party — or a Cacharel fashion show of the period, which was more or less the same thing. Indeed, these shows were orchestrated by Corinne and their poetic symbolism was profoundly marked by her artistic sensibility. There was the ballet under the stars of the spring-summer 1970 show, with its Botticelli-like girls parading at the planetarium in the Palais de la Découverte to a soundtrack of Baroque music. Then there was the spring-summer 1971 show in the Cirque d'Hiver. There the catwalk was entirely covered in a Liberty patchwork, and a mixture of children and flower-girls casually finished putting their make-up on in public before wandering endlessly around the stage in a light, inventive way, to the folk guitar sounds of Valérie Lagrange.

The exhilarating memory of this beautiful adventure with Liberty remains very vivid for Corinne Sarrut: "There was so much enthusiasm and everything was so easy. Everything just flowed from the source. I created what I wanted to wear, everybody went along with it and it sold. We could turn something that was perfectly natural to me into a success. It was light, spontaneous, pleasing, we believed in it.[1]" Sarah Moon echoes these sentiments: "We were keen, we were fearless, everything succeeded...[3]" Sarah Moon! She was the person who made the image the inimitable hallmark of Cacharel.

She was a model. A model, one day she had wanted to try her hand at photography, just for the fun of going to "the other side of the

15

looking glass," of seeing rather than being seen. From the outset, she proved to be one of those rare artists who has the ability to project their own image and soul into their work. In her bedroom, transformed into an impromptu studio, she posed her closest friends, a small clan of people who were passionately interested in the same things. They were slightly rebellious, a little at odds with their times. They spent their vacations at Formentera and dreamed of themselves in terms of mysticism and romantic nostalgia. Corinne Sarrut was part of this group and she introduced Sarah to her brother-in-law.

Jean Bousquet was still on the lookout for new talent to give his intuitions concrete form. He was able at the right time to rediscover the Liberty fabric and entrust Corinne Sarrut with the task of turning it into a fashion object. Now he was certain that Sarah Moon was the right person to create an image for it. He gave her carte blanche.

Cacharel, Corinne Sarrut, Sarah Moon — as André Breton would have put it, this was "incidental magic."

S arah Moon became Cacharel's creator of images. Her friendship and collaboration with Corinne Sarrut made things easy, without however removing their differences. Sarah says as much today: "Corinne clothed her double, while I identified with the woman that I was photographing...[3]"

Corinne created dresses for a dreamy, fragile woman, a woman-child who was similar to her. It was charming, but Sarah went further. She took her friend's creations and imbued them with the full weight of her unconscious and her memory — the memory of an English childhood, with the smell of tea in floral china. It was an unreal, delightful but terrifying world, redolent of the tales illustrated by Arthur Rackham, the disturbing charm of *Alice in*

Wonderland, the desperate romanticism of the Bronte sisters and the Pre-Raphaelite gentleness of Ophelia drowned amid the waterlilies.

Focusing her fantasies on Liberty, she succeeded in endowing this incarnation of fashion devoted to the ephemeral with a hint of the eternal and, above and beyond that, in revealing through her photographs the very color of Cacharel's soul.

She was able to achieve this because her world was not that of fashion, but that of fiction and the imagination. She never photographed clothes, but rather the women wearing them — or, to be more precise, she created a script for these women, a décor that was as carefully worked out as the composition of a painting. Perhaps a story would emerge from it? In short, the subjects were "characters in search of an author," an author who could not be them. Sarah let herself be guided by chance. Suddenly, there would be a quiver and a little dramatic scene would emerge. Sarah captured on film these fleeting moments of an entire world that she had invented.

Thanks to the magic of Sarah Moon, Cacharel and Liberty would always be part of this dream world, at the frontiers of the real, on the edge of suspended time. There was an atmosphere of whispered secrets, bonds forming, a world of women among themselves, evanescent, gentle women who were always slightly mysterious and who seemed to want to linger in the nostalgic romanticism of an adolescence that was still close. With their childlike curls and porcelain complexions, the childish gravity of their faces with their rosy doll-like cheeks, the hollow eyes of people lost in a forgotten dream, their tiny mouths painted in the shape of cherries, they looked like little girls playing at being women. But behind this regression, this return to innocence, throbbed a veiled eroticism, perhaps also the beguiling fear of being confronted with love for the first time.

From one collection to the next, Liberty became a pretext for harmonious images in which the secret links between the poses, lines, soft colors and the light created a certain grace.

Sarah Moon writes with light.

A woman is sitting in the half-light in a rattan rocking chair. Her floral dress is pretty, but is hard to make out. The only things that are lit are the eyes lost in reverie set in a pale face and the two hands resting on the armrests. Is she waiting? Reminiscing? *Chi lo sa!*

Elsewhere, a very vague elsewhere of female intimacy, three sisters are making themselves look beautiful for some party or other. The luminous rectangles of a window splash across the Liberty dresses. But only the gestures of complicity, the light touch of fingers, the sketchy movements have a presence.

Two friends doze next to each other during a siesta. The bodies hardly touch each other. The ample dresses with their pleats overlap in a large expanse of fabric which spreads everywhere, framing the slumbering forms. It resembles an immense monochrome patchwork in which the browns of the motifs on the fabric merges with the red of the hair. As in a Klimt painting, there are no blank spaces. And yet the fabric disappears; we forget about it. All that remains is the mystery lurking under the closed eyelids.

everything is suggested, unspoken, sketched out. Yet the evocative power and the suggestiveness of these visual and poetic reveries about Cacharel are extremely potent. By allowing each woman to appropriate each scene so that she can graft her own story onto it, the images created by Sarah Moon generate an irresistible desire to enter for ever into the world of Cacharel. It is a bit like a magic mirror over which you merely need to lean in order to pass, according to your mood, from the role of *ingénue* to that of a more ambiguous woman.

Jean Bousquet, by situating himself in a dream world in this way, by deliberately taking the risk of adopting a visual approach in which the product disappeared for the benefit of the picture, became a pioneer of a new genre. Nobody before him had thought of making imagery the very heart of the brand's identity. At the end of the Sixties, he was the first person to develop, with the aid of a progressive advertising manager, Robert Delpire (Sarah Moon's husband), a radically new brand concept in which a type of imagery that was instantly recognizable replaced the word and the garment, by creating a mood, an atmosphere. And it was in the wake of this Impressionistic approach that, from 1978, such perfumes as Anaïs Anaïs and Loulou were created. Advertisements, posters, catalogues, invitation cards, packaging — everything was produced in the same brand spirit, creating a complete unity of approach.

More than anything else, the magical power of the image explains why people formed such strong bonds with the brand. Sarah Moon's evocative imaginary world literally sprayed the world of women with the Esprit Cacharel, and the wider world as well. Once, at the height of the disco craze, in a cinema screening *Grease* with John Travolta, the entire audience suddenly got up to applaud the advertisement for *Anaïs Anaïs*. Young women stuck on their bedroom walls the glossy pictures showing the famous packaging and each lived their love story with the brand. Each of them nurtured the dream of following *Loulou* in her dance as she flies off to join Cacharel.

Notes

1. Interview of Corinne Sarrut, Paris, 2001–2002.
2. "*Prêt-à-porter* spring 1974", Hélène de Turckheim, *Le Figaro*, 25 October 1973.
3. Interview of Sarah Moon, Paris, 2001–2002.

Chronology

1958: Jean Bousquet, born in Nîmes and a qualified tailor, starts up a small business making trousers for women from a single room in the Rue Saintonge in Paris.

1962: Jean Bousquet, whose workshop is now located 9, Rue des Fontaines-du-Temple, registers the brand "Jean Cacharel," clothes designer (trousers, skirts and blouses). "Cacharel" is French for a Camargue teal, a choice of name intended as a homage to Bousquet's Provençal origins.

1963: First *Elle* cover with the famous pink blouse, the "Cacharel," worn by a star cover girl of the time, Nicole de Lamargé, photographed by Peter Knapp.

1964: Jean Bousquet moves his business to 18-20, Rue du Faubourg-du-Temple and on December 1, 1964 founds the limited liability company "Jean Cacharel" (business: sportswear ready-to-wear), which in 1965 would become a limited company. This was the period of the collections created by the designer Emmanuelle Khanh.

1965: Summer : The "chemisier crépon" becomes all the rage.

1966: Opening of the first production plant in Nîmes. October : Corinne Sarrut is hired as a designer by Jean Bousquet. On Saint Catherine's day, a presentation/happening is held in Rue Princesse, with the participation of Jean-Marie Rivière and famous racing car drivers Jean-Pierre Beltoise and Johnny Servoz-Gavin.

1968: Start of the collaboration with Sarah Moon. First Liberty blouses. First designs for men. Gérard Grandval designs the famous futuristic offices in the Rue du Faubourg-du-Temple for Cacharel. They were used as a set in the film *Slogan* by Pierre Grimblat with Serge Gainsbourg and Jane Birkin.

1969: First designs for children. First color posters. Creation by Robert Delpire of the famous Cacharel logo. October: Valéry Giscard d'Estaing, Minister of Finance, presents Jean Bousquet with the Oscar for Exports. Cacharel is the first ready-to-wear company to receive the award.

1970: *Elle* selects Jean Cacharel as one of the "60 top Frenchmen who have marked the decade." First Cacharel dresses in Liberty (spring-summer collection).

1971: Cacharel takes part in the twin exhibitions "Design Français" and "Vêtements Fonctionnels" presented at the Centre de Création industrielle à l'Union centrale des arts décoratifs. The autumn-winter 1971-72 collection "French Follies" travels to several French cities. October: Donna Jordan, a member of Andy Warhol's circle, and the model Pat Cleveland "direct themselves" for Cacharel during the presentation of the spring-summer 1972 collection "Pavane pour un dimanche d'été."

1972: Sarah Moon shoots the film *Pavane pour un dimanche d'été.*

An important moment: The choice of Liberty samples in the offices of Jean Bousquet, Rue du Faubourg du Temple. He is wearing a Liberty tie, and Corrine Sarrut a Cacharel "Matilda" print (daisies and poppies). 1968. © Lipnitsky/Roger-Viollet.

1973: First advertising for men's clothing with a poster on the Champs-Elysées showing giant shirts in thermoform plastic. October: Presentation of the Spring-Summer 1974 collection with tap-dancing. It closes with a bird man inspired by the world of Sarah Moon.

1975: The Cacharel boutique "Vog" opens in Paris at 34, Rue Tronchet, designed by Gérard Grandval (clothes, Liberty fabrics sold by the meter, first Mod's Hair salon with robes in Liberty fabric, stationery, tearoom, etc.). Arrival of the designer Junko Shimada for the children's collection. First Lafayette collection. First licensing contract in Japan.

1976: Summer: The great Liberty period; sales of Liberty fabrics at Cacharel reach almost one million meters. To mark the centenary of Liberty's, Cacharel creates an exclusive collection for the Galeries Lafayette. Winter: First national advertising campaign in bus shelters (women's men's and children's clothing).

1977: Cacharel is the top French exporter in the clothing sector. Art Kane takes the company's advertising for menswear in a new direction.

1978: Anaïs Anaïs, Cacharel's first perfume, is created in collaboration with L'Oréal. Registered office transferred to 49, Rue Etienne-Marcel.

1979: At the Cannes Festival, Sarah Moon wins the Grand Prix for best international advertising film for her Cacharel films Femme and Enfant.

1981: Launch of the perfume Cacharel pour l'Homme. Anaïs Anaïs is the best-selling women's perfume in the world. *Stratégies* awards Cacharel first prize for advertising.

1982: Cacharel is twenty years old. Making of the film *Joyeux anniversaire* by Marianne Lamour. Cacharel is the top French women's ready-to-wear company.

1986: Gold Lion in Cannes for *Casting*, advertising film by Sarah Moon.

1987: Launch of Loulou, Cacharel's second women's perfume. Gold Lion in Cannes for Loulou, an advertising film by Sarah Moon.

1994: Creation of a new women's perfume, Eden.

1998: Creation of "the wonder perfume" Noa, which in 1999 received the FIFI award for the "Best European Perfume."

2000: Arrival of the design duo Clements Ribeiro, graduates of St Martin's School of Art. October: Spring-Summer 2001 collection, the first to be designed by Clements Ribeiro, is presented at the Louvre.

2002: Launch of Gloria, Cacharel's latest perfume. "Gloria, unique and various, Gloria or the thousand faces of femininity."

Gloria. The last emblematic heroine of the Cacharel perfumes. Publicity shot.© Photograph Warren du Preez & Nick Thornton-Jones-Air Paris.

Cacharel

Paris, 1968, Rue du Faubourg-du-Temple. Jean Bousquet, creator of the Jean Cacharel imprint, poses with a model in his futuristic office suite, the work of Gérard Grandval. © Lipnitski/Roger-Viollet.

Corinne Sarrut wearing one of her favorite creations, the Liberty dress, and an ingenue's wistful expression framed by a straw hat with a turned-up border from which two schoolgirl braids protrude. The Gigi look incarnate. © Personal Archive, Corinne Sarrut.
1980. Twin sisters in the Luxembourg Gardens. Laurence and Valérie wear the same Cacharel bird print. © Sarah Moon.

Robe-sarrau accessorized with a very 1920s flowered cloche. Contrast comes from Liberty print on the breast pocket and along the V-neck. Marie Claire, April 1974. © SIC/Nama Rein.
Small-flowered Liberty print for this very Claudine à l'école dress with pleated front, round collar, and balloon sleeves. It's modeled by Isabelle Weingarten, Wim Wenders's future muse. Elle, May 12, 1975. © Elisabeth Novick/Scoop-Elle.

Liberty dress. Bare back, butterfly sleeves, and narrow-pleated skirt. Elle, June 3, 1974. © William Connors/Scoop-Elle.
The same dress on the runway at the Cacharel spring-summer 1974 show, Rue du Faubourg-du-Temple. © Meunier/Sipa Press.

Parad 1974. "The Bird Man," a giant poster by Sarah Moon, provides a backdrop to two Liberty dresses. They're light, roomy, with slightly puffed long sleeves, worn with Bonnie and Clyde-style berets and Salomés. Timeless freshness. © Meunier/Sipa Press.
Fall-Winter 2002. Celia Birtwell, muse to David Hockney and creator of fashion fabrics for Ossie Clark, designed for Cacharel the exclusive "Leaves" print on these jersey skirts. © Jessica Bousquet.

A natural, romantic, pastoral scene: Corinne Sarrut is joined by her daughter Agathe and Camille Grandval, who wears sabots and a long skirt. April 1971. © SIC/Galland.
A winter Liberty, but very lighthearted, this clinging minidress has tight sleeves, narrow bust, pleated miniskirt. Marie Claire, January 1971. © SIC/Kent.

The hippie finale of the Cacharel Summer-Spring 1970. Palais de la Découverte, Paris. Barefoot, crowned with flowers, women. Collection at the children circled under the heavenly dome of the planetarium. © Personal archives, Corinne Sarrut.

The gypsy dress from summer 1970. Round decolletage, tight waist, narrow sleeves, long skirt gathered up, long-waisted, once again with delicate Liberty flowers, in soft, bright tints, set off against navy blue. © Alain Vivier /20 ans, March 1970.

Balthus, *La Patience,* 1954-55, Maurice Rheims collection, Paris. Possibly one of the keys to the Cacharel spirit. © Adagp, Paris, 2002.

In a very Cacharel kind of setting, Sarah Moon writes with light. Spring-Summer Collection 1974. © Sarah Moon.

Summer 1974, the summer of Cacharel and Liberty. Sharing the sweet intimacy of feminine secrets, three sisters prepare for a special party. © Sarah Moon.

Cacharel beauties in ultra-feminine chemisier dress, floral print on silk viscose, pastel shades, leg-of-mutton sleeves, small officer's collar or wide pleated neckpiece. Collection Autumn-Winter 1974. © Sarah Moon.

A "camouflage" theme dominates this photograph: In a "Japanese landscape" Liberty print, a pouting, self-confident Lolita-type becomes the central theme of the wall mosaic that serves as backdrop. *Elle,* June 8, 1970. © Peter Knapp.
A return to innocence, or perverse coquettishness? Disturbing ambiguity surrounds this child-woman in a Liberty minidress with modest long sleeves and an ultra-short pleated skirt. *Vogue,* February 1971. © Jeanloup Sieff.

Alice's Adventures in Wonderland illustrated by Arthur Rackham, 1907. One facet of Sarah Moon's English inspiration. © Christie's Images/Bridgeman Giraudon. "The Arthur Rackham pictures are reproduced with the kind permission of his family".
A Jumeau doll from 1900? Alice in Wonderland? This child, pretending to be a woman, has had her hand decorated with pink nail polish, a nice contrast to the blue Liberty print of an apron dress that recalls the Belle Epoque. 1979. © Sarah Moon.

"Once upon a time," Mr. Cat recites to this girl in a cinnamon Liberty dress with embroidered collar and insertion. *Vogue*, august 1978. © Sarah Moon.

Beauty and the Beast, or the ballet in which the birdman carries off the lady fresh as a rosebud in her Cacharel dress. Collection spring-summer 1974. One more demonstration of Sarah Moon's passion for fantasy and dreamlike settings. © Sarah Moon.

A country flavor surrounds this harmonious arrangement in navy and white cotton: flowered shirt and apron dress with large blossoms, semi-long skirt and wide pockets. This mix of prints is totally Cacharel 75. *Elle*, February 17, 1975. © T. Donovan/Scoop-*Elle*.
Botticelli hairstyle by Mod's Hair goes well with this Cacharel Liberty dress from winter 1970-71. *Marie Claire*, January 1971. © SIC/Kent.

Winter 1969. "Jazz," a Liberty print for this silk chemisier. This was the first time a Liberty was featured so prominently in a Cacharel collection. Peter Knapp won the 1969 Nikon Black and White Prize. © Peter Knapp.

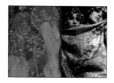

Gustav Klimt, *Water Snakes II,* 1904-07. An aquatic dream in which hair, algae, and flowers blend and interlace. © Galerie Welz, Salzburg.
Invitation to the Cacharel Spring-Summer 1969 show. This was one of Sarah Moon's first designs for Cacharel. The two models huddle beneath a patchwork of fabrics from the collection. © Sarah Moon.

An atmosphere reminiscent of a Russian baba, again with Liberty for these long pleated skirts in wool with coordinated scarf. Autumn-Winter Collection 1974-75. © Sarah Moon.

A great cameo patchwork in which the browns of the Liberty patterns blend with the auburn hair. There's not one inch of empty space. And yet the scarf is unobtrusive, overlooked; we're left with only an enigma behind closed eyelids. Cacharel, Autumn-Winter Collection 1976-77. © Sarah Moon.

Invitation card for the presentation of the Cacharel Autumn-Winter 1969-70. Collection at the restaurant Le Train Bleu. © Sarah Moon.

"Calypso" print by Celia Birtwell for dress and top in double georgette crêpe. Cacharel, Spring-Summer 2003 Collection. © Jessica Bousquet.

Susan Moncur, a famous model of the 1970s and '80s, in a Cacharel ensemble: antique-rose pleated skirt with broad flowers, bordeaux Jacquard cardigan, white for the beret, the crêpe chemisier, and the greyhound, with the accent, a bit diabolic perhaps, of a red chiffon scarf loosely thrown around the neck. The mood is a little uneasy. Shades of Mia Farrow in Roman Polanski's *Rosemary's Baby*. Spring-Summer Collection 1975. © Sarah Moon.

To honor the Cacharel twentieth anniversary, Sarah Moon invented the woman-bouquet, bordering on a Surrealist dream, woman as object of metamorphosis. Cacharel, invitation to the anniversary dinner on March 30, 1982. © Sarah Moon.

Spring-Summer 2003 Collection. Gored skirt in cotton crepe. Oversized jersey top in striped cotton. © Friedemann Hauss.
Silk crepe top in Celia Birwell's "Alhambra" print from the Spring-Summer 2003 Collection, with a pleated skirt lined with *georgette* silk with bayadere stripes. © Friedemann Hauss.

The author would like to thank everyone who through their support, their accounts and their advice have contributed greatly to the preparation of this book.

She would like in particular to express her gratitude to Jean and Dominique Bousquet, Sarah Moon, Corinne Sarrut and all those who worked for Cacharel and Martine Assouline.

She would also like to thank Jessica Bousquet and Frédérique Stumpf for their efficient help.

She would like to express her gratitude to all those who were active in the 1960s and 1970s and who were kind enough to agree to being interviewed: Maïmé Arnodin, Nicole Bamberger, Annegret Beier, Elisabeth Bernigaud, Célia Bertin, Lison Bonfils, Dominique Brabec, Jean-Charles Brosseau, Claude Brouet, Gilles de Bure, Richard Cooper, Nicole Crassat, Nina Dausset, Claude Finet, Susan Fletcher, Nadine Gasc, Gérard Grandval, Didier Grumbach, Elie and Jacqueline Jacobson, Emmanuelle Khanh, Peter Knapp, Arlette Lacour, Catherine Lardeur, Marie-José Lepicard, Annette Luit, Franka de Mailly, Noémie Mainguet, Marianne Milliès-Lacroix, Alice Morgaine, Annie Mouratille, Harri Peccinotti, Colette Roussaux, Gilbert Saada, Ginette Sainderichin, Julius Schofield, Anne-Marie Seznec, Françoise Vincent-Ricard and the late Melka Treanton.

This book also owes much to Laure Sérullaz at Editions Assouline and to the support provided during research by Annie Barbera, Sylvie Roy (Musée de la Mode de le Ville de Paris, Musée Galliera), Emmanuelle Montet, Marie-Hélène Poix (Musée de la Mode et du Textile), Pascale Le Cacheux (Musée des Tissus and Musée des Arts Décoratifs de Lyon) and Gérald Chevalier.

Finally, she would like to express her heartfelt thanks to Marc Audibet, who helped her formulate her ideas about Cacharel with such intuition, and to Françoise Auguet and Mage Barbier for their invaluable advice and their kind support.

The publisher would like to thank the Comtesse Klossowski von Rola and the Fondation Balthus at Rossinière in Switzerland, Maître Maurice Rheims, Léo Scheer, Olivier Monteil (L'Oréal), Jean-Pierre Cap (Sarah Moon), Marina Rotondo (Skira publishing, Milan), Francis Eck (Roger-Viollet), Sylviane Giraldon and Edith Saadi (Scoop-Elle), Sandrine Kaïm and Béatrice Vidal-Pioli (Marie Claire group), Martine Detier and Véronique Quiquerée (Sipa Press), Elsa Duperrier (Excelsior group), Franz Eder (Galerie Welz at Salzburg in Austria).